Playthings

poems by

Ilan Mochari

Finishing Line Press
Georgetown, Kentucky

Playthings

ACKNOWLEDGMENTS

"The survival secrets of spiders" appeared in *Inkwell*

"Gibbous Reflection" appeared in *J Journal*

"i sugared your sorrows" appeared in *Salamander*

"Playthings" appeared in *Tilde*

"Industrial Park No. 2" appeared in *Specter*

"A request to the new tenant" appeared in *Hobart*

"Station" appeared in *The Minnesota Review*

"Weekday, City" appeared in *So It Goes: The Literary Journal of the Kurt Vonnegut Museum and Library*. It was nominated for a Pushcart Prize

"From the Faraway, Nearby" appeared in *Pamplemousse*

"The Windows Are Too Wide at Starbucks" appeared in *North Dakota Quarterly*

"Fiancé/Fiancée" appeared in *Dash*

"Centerfield" appeared in *Little Patuxent Review*

"5:45 bus" appeared in *Molecule*

Publisher: Leah Huete de Maines
Editor: Christen Kincaid
Cover Art: Whitney Scharer
Author Photo: Joshua Touster
Cover Design: Whitney Scharer

Order online: www.finishinglinepress.com
also available on amazon.com

Author inquiries and mail orders:
Finishing Line Press
PO Box 1626
Georgetown, Kentucky 40324
USA

Contents

To my mother and stepfather

Manilkara zapota elegy (Yucatán Peninsula)

shirtless *chicleros*,
their nostrils ravaged
by jungle flies,
climbed you
& etched zigzags
in your bark,
their machete blades glinting
as resin dripped milky
down your trunk
into watertight bags.

your essence, these men
brought to a shed
to be boiled
& poured into molds,
date-stamped & canvas-bound
in bales of four,
& carried by mule
to Belize's ports.

you are doomed
to be remembered
as the source
of a commercial product,
wrapped in foil
or low-grade paper—

to be a footnote:
once known
as an evergreen
shimmering in ornamental gardens,
your fruit a staple
of bishops' diets,
your wood used for lintels
in Tikal's temples.

The survival secrets of spiders

I.

you emerged from your burrows on a fat new earth:
conifers dotted the land,
hard-winged beetles nibbled on leaves;

you spun collar webs from your rear,

you mixed shimmering filaments with dirt,
hiding behind them for safety,
only coming out at night
when your mate—or your prey—
stepped gingerly nearby,
triggering the strand your pedipalps were touching
in their quest for desired vibrations.

II.

the brown recluse hides in a folded towel and bites a homeowner
in Missouri,
        marking his hairy shin with a crimson crust;

the black widow scampers through trash in Tallahassee,
        living out her years in a funnel-shaped habitat;

the desert loxoscele blends in the sands of the Escalante,
        going three months without water;

the silver argiope spins crisscrossing strands in a Miami
backyard,
        haloing a pink prickly pear;

the bola in the San Antonio suburbs lassoes a moth with her
silken sack,
        rappelling down a strand to kill it;

and the arrowshaped micrathena lays her eggs in the wet woods
of Nebraska,
      depositing them on a yellow leaf;

it's the last act of her yearlong life.

III.

a burrowing spider mother brings her egg sac to the surface,
exposing it to the sun's warmth in the wilderness;
the sac darkens to earthy brown, till it's time for hatching;
her two hundred spiderlings scramble onto her back;

see how they cling, leglocked to each other,
so close, so clasped—a cape
contoured to the mother's back.

they cling when she's meditating at the burrow's bottom,
when she's outside the burrow searching for food
in the low, parched grass of the old park with the sand-moored
swing set;
when the mother darts between wind-whipped blades
seeking prey;

and if any of the babies fall from her,
they seek her jointed legs like flagpoles in the dirt
until they rejoin their siblings within the cape's fabric.

Gibbous Reflection

Astronauts swore the ragged rocks
beneath their boots and the grimy
particles on their space suits
were gray as gunpowder, then black
as night sky, your backdrop, back home
(as if a starless ceiling). Yet the whitest
hues—chalky, ghostly, bloodless—
have remained the archetype,
though credentialed scientists have proven
your surface is a broken mirror, crunched
into jags and shards, morphed into
meanings and myths of fertility.

i sugared your sorrows

for ninety-nine cents / *pulpy, stringy, filmy, fibrous*

the first time we were alone / *a texture only you have felt*

after the dust speck inside you / *particle, granule, miniscule, needlepoint*

spilled out, slapping toilet water / *michaelmas term lately over*

a discharge of bloody yolk / *you quipped composedly*

a pebble's plash / *before sending me out*

belying lasting grief / *to buy you some peanut butter cups*

Playthings

kiss me the liquid, the whiteknuckled yank,
the clenching and spray of mate fleet and surprising.
throw my leg high,
higher;
tally at my pace your skims,
dancing like stones on the sand-slapping ocean.
honor my hieroglyph'd helix now ours:
i rise, roll, slide, tilt, shift, and twist,
i stretch, stagger, and buckle,
my minor groove becomes a major one.
move to me, let me chew your lips;
sustain my illusion of a union undying,
a chemistry that makes playthings
of nations, extinctions, and war.

Recidivism, or Why I Ate the Entire Pint

Discipline's death, existential excuses
flood the basement of your brain:
spackled cracks yield to torrents, and you
blame Camus, not the clouds. The entry
for hunger in your synonym finder
ought to say hedonism.
Such is your privacy's passion.

From the Faraway, Nearby

Take me, docent, to the surreal O'Keeffe,
Where a liminal desert & mountainous sands
Set a brown, jawless skull in abandoned relief.
Bones bloom like blessings from holier lands,
Antlers curl Godward like six withered hands
Or calligraphic Hebrew, draped in the sky,
Near cloud wisps stripped thin by symbolic demands.
As if centuries sidestepping questions of why
Left us only with deer horns to deify.

Docent, lead me to the O'Keeffe eternal,
Where the head of the cervid is floating on high,
As if lifted to heaven by forces maternal.
This canvas depicts, this title affirms
An art in the juxtaposed distance of terms.

Manilkara zapota elegy (Tenochtitlan)

you loomed in forests, one hundred feet tall
bats and thrips enticed by scent and color
abetted your calyx-hemmed flowers
in cycles of nobly loveless reproduction.

Aztec harlots clacked your substance
in the market, announcing themselves to johns;
further east, *bataboʼob* sealed letters with chaws,
containing plans for war.

without you, masticators resorted
to betel nuts, coca leaves,
spermaceti, tobacco,
the cartilage of walrus flippers.

now your sugary exudate
darkens with age,
hardening
to oval-shaped tears;
it lies
flattened on sidewalks,
sticking to wheels of strollers,
enameling inscriptions of fame.

Industrial Park No. 2

I have it on good authority that the man
         who invented these paint-by-number clusters
                was raised not on bedtime stories but zoning
laws.

How best to anatomize this oxymoron
         of commerce, these faux-silver structures
                whose name blasphemes slides and seesaws?

Within walking distance of nothing domestic,
         their humanity comes from workplace subcultures,
                white-collar heroes following stars

in a world that's become a pandemic
         of cars.

A request to the new tenant

Walls bare but for paint & hooks, floors bare but for stains & nails,
we leave insides as we find them; yet of neighbors & gardens
                we have less control. still, you need not care
                        for the backyard plants
                the landlord's mom keeps the weeds in check;

but in the shrubs there's a rabbit who comes to live here
every spring—and i fancied
                myself its secret caretaker:

i brought it peeled organic baby carrots & bowls
of chilled spring water & watched its small head of light brown fur
                bob up & down as it hopped from its
                        hiding space in the shrubs
                & chewed on the meal i'd prepared;

it never asked me to come inside or judged me for not
extending an invitation. it was
                        in the shrubs four years ago
                when i first moved here, newly divorced;

it was in the shrubs two years ago when i first slept
with the man i'm now moving in with; and it was
                in the shrubs on the june night
                        when my stepfather called—
                late for him to be calling, i thought;
strange for him, not mom, to be calling.

one day later we buried her.
& when i came back here i found my rabbit
                in front of the house, as if it knew
                        everything i'd been through.

are your folks alive? i thought so. you look young.

i don't mean to dump my life story on your lap.

just please
don't get alarmed if you see me
in the shrubs some sunday, either
                with my guy or on my own. i am
                prematurely nostalgic
for my old pal, the light brown rabbit.

we've been through so much, through the years,
& i just want it to know
that this farewell
is not nothing,
& it is not for good

Station

In the weedy yard where the city stored light rail trains I mounted
my camera on a tripod and waited hours for winter images
worthy of my 36 exposures. Drivers drank from thermoses
and flirted, tugging each other's bright green vests, lighting
each other's cigarettes. One by one they climbed into vehicles,
switching on *next stop* announcements. Folding doors squeaked
shut; trains hummed, rolling toward faregates.

Whenever I needed to reset my eyes I gazed at slices of cloud,
at cardinals circling the bare-branched sugar maples, at gabled
dormers of municipal buildings. Snow conquered curbs below.
Flakes froze in hip-high piles, streaked with dirt specks and
urine. I sought sublimities in their filthy layers.

A strange sound—crepitant, destructive, like a blender stuck on
a pit—snapped me from my trance. I looked up from my lens to
the canopied platform, where a man in a vest was trying to sweep
a squirrel carcass into an upright dustpan. At first the carcass did
not fit the rectangular receptacle; the man resorted to wedging
and ramming, prodding and pressing, until the echo of the
dustpan scraping on asphalt was the only evidence of struggle. He
jogged to the nearest trash bin and emptied it there, staring at the
sky as he did so, as if to say, *forgive me, you who maybe saw this.*

Fiancé/Fiancée

blade by right nipple, rabbi slits my shirt
cotton shrieks amidst mourners' whispers
none of these mourners saw how it happened
they whisper not of what i told the police,
shouting through sirens as they chewed their gum
and scribbled their notes:
her bike got caught
between a bus and parked Subaru
suddenly opening its driver side door
i was riding behind her. she was
(and i am) twenty-four.
hand on her casket, i steady myself,
imagine my lungs bursting
through the carved-out hole in my dress shirt.
rabbi completes the memorial prayer,
inviting bereaved persons to speak.
stop whispering! i scream, running out of the room.

Shriving

When red claps briny & thorns prick beer,
Whispering iris, kisses of salt,
Edges of lower teeth cleaning a nail,
Scraping your palms creasing taste of the fear,
Wringing the sponge by its lemony tail,
Gasping gills, porous, he thinks it's your fault.

When blue smacks dewy & waves whack a lung,
Curling from foam soapy amorous tongue,
Swipe the stick, tamp it, it slides through your lips,
Doctrine explicit spontaneous quips,
Silk strands, spinnerets, younger-you stories,
Cutting corollas, mourning your glories,
Why to the lake of your childhood, driven?
Parents, exes, you thought you'd forgiven.

Weekday, City

The jacketless teen in laceless, snow-soaked boots paces the sidewalk,
to the corner and back, to the corner and back,
whistling, squatting, leaping at intervals,
observed but ignored by the commuters,
whose faces are hidden by hats and scarves.
Headlights dot the dark as the bus approaches,
its thick tires mashing gutter-lodged ice blocks.
When the sooty doors hiss open, the commuters line up behind him,
their gloved fingers strangling their fare cards.

In the third-grade classroom, where fluorescents hum high overhead,
a hairless, heavy student sketches football schemes in the margins of
his workbook.
His thick fingers wield the pencil with an unorthodox grip,
the kind that would've been corrected in bygone days,
before the blackboard clacks of broken-chalk taps
were replaced by the whiteboard of soft-tipped silence.
Like a video game savant who never needs to look down at his
controller,
for the controller is one with his hands, eyes, and brain,
this eight-year-old draws plays that would be the envy of college
coaches.
Formations, alignments, and motions are like his mother tongue,
Xs and Os his alphabet.
His classmates ridicule him at recess;
they're too young to savor the sap
of a boy who prefers drawing plays to playing.
They envy how the teacher lets him wear his cap during the pledge.

At the restaurant, the chef simmers sliced beets
as sweat drips from his mustache and bandana-clad hair
onto his eight-button coat, which is open at the neck.

Beets slide around the greased-up pan like skateboarders on a vert
ramp,
flying over the lip but always landing within.

Flip phone between his ear and shoulder,
his wife in Venezuela is screaming.
The remittances haven't arrived—the kids have no clothes for
school—
the lawyer needs more cash for visas.
She's okay with his having a wife and kids in the US, too,
but his first family should come first.
He slaps shut the phone and drops it in the baggy pocket of his cotton
pants,
which his US wife bought him for his twenty-first birthday.

On the boulevard, the driver halts the bus between stops—
a frail, familiar passenger has waved him down.
She boards, sits next to the jacketless boy, and tells him she's ninety
years old.

On the back steps of the daycare center, the single mothers embrace;
their third graders, meeting for the first time, trade football cards
with gloved hands.
The able-bodied one asks: How long do you have?
The bald one says: Two years tops.
They agree to trade cards as often as they can in that time.

At the church's dinner for the homeless,
volunteers fill three-gallon dispensers with scalding coffee,
fold paper napkins into triangles,
and serve a stew of chorizo, potatoes, and pink beans.
Now they've eaten, now they're clearing plates, resetting for pudding
and pecan pies.
More coffee, all around! Here come the board games, here come the
decks of cards!

At the gas station the newly married male nurse pumps his bike tires.
Dressed in sky-colored scrubs and a down coat,
he rides from one state-owned building to the next.
The dry-lipped residents smile as he enters their apartments.

Help me climb into the bath—come back later to pull me out!
Reach high to the top shelf—I need the fifty bucks I keep there for
scratch tickets.
Son, what are your lucky numbers?
And how old are you anyway? Thirty-six?
I have a granddaughter who's thirty-two, but you're married—so
forget it!

Some mute their TVs when he comes in, some change the channel;
some receive more drugs than they need, bragging about it to
neighbors.
Some wheel oxygen tanks from room to room,
others sit on couch cushions dented and stained;
some enjoy the community of the building, others detest it:
they envy those with wealth and health enough
to breathe out their days on terms more private and rarified.

Near the state-owned building, in the chef's apartment,
where nine other restaurant workers live,
a new tenant, age fourteen, arrives in dirty clothes,
seeking the chef, repeating *trabajo* to everyone he meets.
The chef tells the two youngest workers to make room on their
mattress
and give the new arrival some clean clothes—
he starts as a busboy tomorrow.

Manilkara zapota elegy (Oaxaca)

chewers, chant her a flattering goodbye;

hers is a legacy scattered by hungry carriers:

kinkajous, opossums & tapirs grabbed her fruit & wandered
elsewhere to eat it;

snout-nosed bats, lured by musty scents, hung in clumps below her
branches,
their necklines dusty with protein-rich grains;

thrips noshed on her leaves, sucking nutrients through their stylets
while pollen brushed their backs—
they hovered, wings clapping, before drifting away.

The Windows Are Too Wide at Starbucks

The sun found a screen backed by silver
and lapsarian fruit. A stuffed koala named Claire,

seated on the sticky table like an ancient god
or statue thereof, did not respond

when the glare blinded her owner
who stomped his sandaled foot. (Muffin crumbs scattered.)

His thousand lines of code he could no longer see,
which felt like a programmer's tragedy.

He squared his shoulders to the pane,
yanking the lift cord with a palm whose lines

augured solitude or romance, depending
on which mystic he consulted on which evening.

The curtain crashed to the cobwebbed sill,
toppling his latte and dousing the marsupial.

He hauled his silver-backed screen to safety
atop a stack of highchairs covered in macaroni.

And he joked to himself that Claire had been baptized,
till he saw the rebuke in her wet, marbled eyes.

5:45 Bus

Defiers of Hypnos we board
when folding doors hiss open,
muttering commonplaces
to a dozy driver. Transit cards
clack the farebox, petty percussion
in a dirge for daylight, drum-taps
for a dawnless December morn.

We squeeze scarved and jacketed
into seats, tacitly consent
to strangers' hips and elbows
touching our own, silent as siblings
scolded for domestic miscues, crumbs
left unswept, dirt tracked inside.
At this time of year, Mars and Neptune
also appear neighborly,
though they're billions of miles apart.

Centerfield

The white sphere in the sky is my focus,
its spiraling seams, its raised red stitches.
I chase the dirt-rubbed object as it swerves
in stifling, midsummer air. My frowning
hat brim blocks the sun's slanting beams, cleats
dent lush grass, my mitt opens, trapping
the gravity-drunk ball in an instant's whap—
a world of outcomes winnowed to a win
justifying the monomania of pursuit.

At Bellow's Grave

On a plane out of Africa
or crosstown bus somewhere in the Midwest,
from the sensual souls of women and men you
and your protagonists carved a calling.

Generalizations about generations, genders,
ethnicities, you made without sounding alarms.
Ever with nuance, the madding mob
you painted with a ward boss's acuity.

Thug among scholars, scholar among thugs,
you compared arctic lichen to human hearts,
made me hate the handicapped guy
who got laid, found fathoms under couch cushions.

The telescope and outhouse combined
to form, in you, a king of not-so-innocent knocking.
Surely you grasp why, in tribute, I stole a rock from your headstone
instead of placing there one of my own.

Antigravity

We dove and slid in wishful emulation
of athletes, opening denim-string
kneeholes in our jeans. Sometimes we waited
till the last second to save the balloon
from touching the ground, hoping
for credit, *oohs* and *ahs* exclaimed
in rich, broadcaster tenors.

In the fall, dry grass threatened
to stab the taut latex, pop it
like a firecracker. The first burst always
shocked our ears, as if we hadn't noticed
the beige blades beneath our feet;
as if we expected needles
to be spry in response.

Ilan Mochari is the author of the novel *Zinsky the Obscure.* His short stories and poems have appeared in *McSweeney's Quarterly Concern, Salamander, Hobart, J Journal, The Louisville Review, Juked, FOLIO, Valparaiso Fiction Review, North Dakota Review,* and elsewhere. His work has been nominated for multiple Pushcart Prizes.

Instagram: https://www.instagram.com/ilanmochari/
X/Twitter: https://x.com/IlanMochari

www.ingramcontent.com/pod-product-compliance
Lightning Source LLC
Chambersburg PA
CBHW030052100426
42734CB00038B/1461